D1071112

A to Z Russia

BY JUSTINE AND RON FONTES

children's press®

A Division of Scholastic Inc.
New York Toronto London Auckland Sydney
Mexico City New Delhi Hong Kong
Danbury, Connecticut

Consultant: Irina Burns
Series Design: Marie O'Neill
Photo Research: Candlepants Incorporated

The photos on the cover show architectural details of the Resurrection of Christ Church in St. Petersburg (right), a Matreshka doll (bottom right), two Russian boys(bottom middle), and a harp seal pup (left).

Library of Congress Cataloging-in-Publication Data

Fontes, Justine.
  Russia / by Justine and Ron Fontes.   APR 2 3 2004
     p. cm. – (A to Z)
Includes bibliographical references and index.
Contents: Animals – Buildings – Cities – Dress – Exports – Food – Government – History – Important people – Jobs – Keepsakes – Land – Map – Nation – Only in Russia – People – Question – Religion – School and sports – Transportation – Unusual places – Visiting the country – Window to the past – X-tra special things – Yearly festivals – Z – Let's explore more – Meet the author – Words you know.
  ISBN 0-516-24558-9 (lib. bdg.)   0-516-26816-3 (pbk.)
  1. Russia (Federation)—Juvenile literature. [1. Russia (Federation)]
I. Fontes, Ron. II. Title. III. Series.
  DK510.23.F66 2003
  947–dc21
                              2003005839

Contents

Animals

Russia has walruses, lynxes, freshwater seals, and different kinds of deer.

Walruses use their tusks to dig up clams, defend themselves against polar bears, and pull themselves over ice.

Lynx

Reindeer are a type of large deer known as caribou. Female reindeer are the only female deer that grow **antlers**. Many of Russia's reindeer are raised by tribal people. They use them for their milk, meat, and skin. They also use them to farm and carry things.

Russia has another kind of deer called elk. They are large deer with a growth of skin around their neck. Each spring, male elk start growing new antlers. During the fall, males use their antlers to fight over who will mate with the females. They shed their antlers in winter.

Lynxes also live in Russia. They hunt deer and smaller animals in Russia's huge pine forests. They have wide, furry feet for walking on snow. Their short tail is only about five inches (13 cm) long.

Seals in Siberia are the only freshwater seals on Earth.

Zhivotnoe

(zhi-VOHT-noh-yeh)
means animal.

5

This is Red Square. Russia's largest history museum and department store are here.

Buildings

The Great Palace is near St. Petersburg. It is surrounded by parks, fountains, and statues. It was built by Peter the Great.

Russian buildings are known for their bright colors and decoration. For many centuries, Russia was separated from the rest of Europe and Asia. However, in the late 17th century and early 18th century, **Czar** Peter the Great tried to make Russia more modern. He brought European architecture and ideas to Russia.

Tsar'

(ZAR)
is the Russian spelling for Czar.

Moscow

Cities

Moscow is Russia's capital and largest city. As early as A.D. 1147, Moscow was a trading post on the Moscow River.

Moscow has museums, theaters, libraries, and schools, as well as many businesses and factories. The Russian government has its offices in a huge palace called the **Kremlin**, which is next to Red Square.

St. Petersburg is another great city in Russia. It has many beautiful buildings and statues, including one of the world's best art museums, the Hermitage.

Dress

In Russian cities, people dress in European–style clothes. In villages, some people wear traditional clothing. The style is similar to the folk costumes of long ago.

Odezhda

(oh-DEZH-dah)
means clothing.

Russian clothes are both beautiful and warm. There are many different styles of folk costumes. Some are decorated with bright stitching on the neck, sleeves, and hems. People once believed these decorations would protect them from evil spirits.

In the far north, Russian Eskimos and other tribal people wear clothes made from animal fur. They are hand-sewn from the skins of animals that had been eaten by the tribe.

The finest Russian caviar costs almost $500 a can!

Exports

Fun Fact:

Some sturgeons live to be over 150 years old. Many weigh over 1,000 pounds (454 kg).

Russia has more crude oil and natural gas than any country on Earth. There is also a lot of coal. Chemicals, machinery, paper, and wood products are also exported.

The country grows more potatoes than any other country in the world. It produces about one-third of the world's crop. But its most famous food export is **caviar**, a salty treat made from the eggs of large, bony fish called sturgeons.

Russian Berry Tea

WHAT YOU NEED:
- 1/2 cup coarsely chopped raspberries or 1/4 cup raspberry or strawberry jam
- the peel of 1 Granny Smith apple
- 1/4 cup dried cherries
- 2 whole cloves
- 4 peppermint tea bags
- 4 cups boiling water

HOW TO MAKE IT:
Place raspberries (or jam), dried cherries, cloves, and tea bags in a large teapot or sauce pan. Add boiling water. Stir. Cover and let steep for 5–10 minutes. Strain and pour into cups. If wanted, add more hot water.

Food

Russians eat lots of bread, potatoes, and soup. One of their favorite soups is **borsch**, which is made from beets. They also drink lots of tea. It is often sweetened with jam instead of sugar.

Ask an adult to help you make some Russian berry tea using this recipe.

11

Russia's parliament building is nicknamed "the White House."

Government

Peter the Great ruled Russia from age 10 until his death at age 53.

Vladimir V. Putin was elected president in March 2000.

The Russian government has a president, a prime minister, and a parliament. Every four years, Russians 18 and older vote to elect a new president. The president appoints the prime minister.

During **Soviet** rule, the **Communist** Party was the only legal political party. In 1985, Mikhail Gorbachev became head of the Communist Party. Gorbachev worked to bring Russia more freedom. Now there are many different political parties in Russia.

Nicholas II was Russia's last Czar. He and his family were killed in 1918.

Joseph Stalin was the leader of Russia's Communist Party.

History

Russia has over 1,000 years of history. During that time many different people settled the land. For 400 years, Russia was ruled by czars. Some czars were good and ruled wisely. Many were cruel and greedy. The **peasants** in Russia suffered for many years.

Russia was a communist country. People voted to change the government in 1991. Now the country is called the Russian Federation.

Marc Chagall was born in Russia in 1887. He also lived in France and the United States.

I and the Village,
by **Marc Chagall, 1911.**

Important People

Russia has inspired many writers and painters. Russian ballet dancers are also among the finest in the world.

Nijinsky was a great Russian actor and dancer.

Born a count (a nobleman), Tolstoy founded a school for peasant children.

Leonid Andreyev was one of many Russian writers inspired by Tolstoy. He wrote short stories and novels.

Leo Tolstoy wrote two of the most famous novels, or long stories, in the world: *War and Peace* and *Anna Karenina*. He served in the Russian Army, then wrote against war.

Marc Chagall was another artist. He painted images of Russian village life. Jewish folklore and Bible stories also inspired Chagall's work.

Vaslav Nijinsky was one of the greatest male dancers. He was famous not only for his leaps, but his ability to become whatever part he played. Nijinsky produced two classic ballets: "Afternoon of a Faun" and "Rite of Spring."

Russia has many industries based on natural resources like coal.

Jobs

Dvigatel'
(DVEE-goh-tel)
is an engine.

For many centuries, most Russians were poor peasants who worked for rich **landlords**. Today, many Russians work in factories building heavy machines like tractors. They also make electronic equipment, chemicals, steel, ships, cars, and processed food. Mining is another big industry.

Russians are now allowed to own their own businesses, like restaurants and taxi services.

This man is playing a *balalaika*.

Keepsakes

You can buy fur hats from street vendors in Moscow.

You can find **balalaikas** in Russia. They look like guitars. They come in different sizes and are played by plucking the strings with the fingers.

You'll also find warm hats called **ushankas**. Ushankas have flaps that can be tied on top or pulled down to cover the ears. These hats are made of real or fake fur.

Like most of Siberia, the Kamchatka Peninsula has very few people or buildings. But there are 28 active volcanoes!

Land

Russia is the largest country on Earth. It is almost twice as big as Canada, the second largest country.

The tallest mountain in Europe is in Russia's Caucasus Mountains.

Russia is very close to the Arctic Circle, which is at the top of the world. Snow covers over half of Russia for six months every year.

Siberia is the coldest part of Russia. The largest flat area in the world is the Central Siberian Plateau. It is over a million square miles.

Russia has many mountains, lakes, and rivers. Many songs and stories have been written about the Volga River, but it is not as big as some of the rivers in Siberia. The Ob and Lena Rivers in Siberia are so wide that people cannot see across them!

Reka

(ree-KAH)
means river.

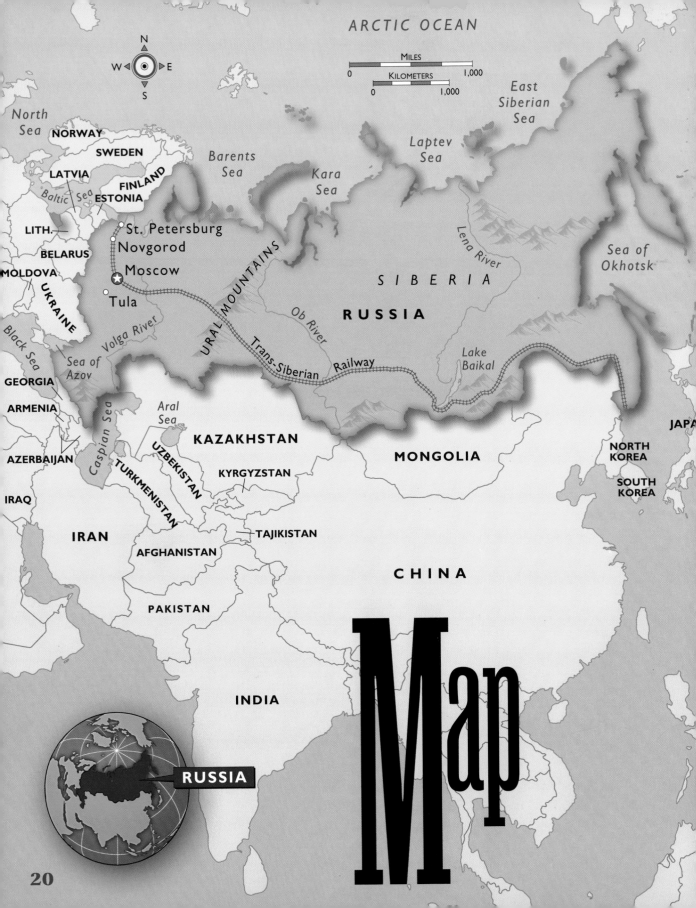

ARCTIC OCEAN

East
Siberian
Sea

*Laptev
Sea*

*Barents
Sea*

*Kara
Sea*

*North
Sea*

NORWAY

SWEDEN

LATVIA

Baltic Sea

FINLAND

ESTONIA

LITH.

BELARUS

MOLDOVA

UKRAINE

St. Petersburg

Novgorod

Moscow

Tula

Volga River

URAL MOUNTAINS

Lena River

S I B E R I A

R U S S I A

*Sea of
Okhotsk*

Ob River

Trans-Siberian   Railway

*Lake
Baikal*

*Black
Sea*

*Sea of
Azov*

GEORGIA

ARMENIA

AZERBAIJAN

IRAQ

IRAN

Caspian Sea

*Aral
Sea*

TURKMENISTAN

UZBEKISTAN

KAZAKHSTAN

KYRGYZSTAN

TAJIKISTAN

AFGHANISTAN

PAKISTAN

MONGOLIA

NORTH
KOREA

SOUTH
KOREA

JAPA

CHINA

INDIA

RUSSIA

MILES

0   1,000

KILOMETERS

0   1,000

N
W   E
S

Map

Nation

During its long history, Russia has had many different flags. Often those flags have used the colors red, white, and blue. In ancient times, the white meant honor. Blue meant purity. Red meant bravery. Later, red stood for the Russian people. Blue stood for the czar. White stood for God. Finally, the blue stood for the Ukraine and the white stood for Belorussia. The people of Belorussia are sometimes called "White Russians."

Trans-Siberian express train

Only in Russia

In 1891, Czar Alexander III began building the Trans-Siberian Railroad. He wanted the railroad to be built by Russian people using Russian materials.

You can see the Trans-Siberian railway from space.

For 12 cold years, workers built the railroad. Finally, in 1916, the Trans-Siberian became the longest railroad line in the world. It still is!

The Trans-Siberian paved the way for future Russian achievements, such as the space program. It proved the skill of their engineers and workers, and the power the Russian people had when they worked together.

People

Many different kinds of people live in Russia. Some of the oldest people in the world live in the Caucasus Mountains. Many live to be over 100 years old.

Narody

(nah-ROH-dee)
people who live
in the country

Liudi

(LOO-dee)
people who live
in the cities

Most Russians are Slavic. There are also Asians, Eskimos, Gypsies, Turks, Greeks, and more.

Russian is the official language, but Polish, Bulgarian, Slovak, and many other languages are spoken.

About three-quarters of the population live in cities. There are many modern high-rise buildings with small apartments. People live in small houses in towns and villages. Some people have country summer homes called **dachas**.

Question Who Was Anastasia?

Anastasia was the youngest daughter of Russia's last czar, Nicholas Romanov. Not long after the **revolution**, Nicholas, his wife, and five children were shot by soldiers. But did one of the children survive?

Years later, many women claimed to be Anastasia. The rest of the Romanov family did not recognize any of these women. But that did not stop the stories from growing. It also inspired many books and films, but historians now know Anastasia died with the rest of her family.

Religion

During Soviet rule, religion was outlawed. Many priests and monks were put in jail. Some churches were destroyed or turned into museums. People worshipped in secret.

In the Russian Federation, people have the freedom of religion. The majority are Russian Orthodox Christians. The second most popular religion is Islam. There are also some Jewish people, Buddhists, and Protestants.

Domes, shaped like onions, top the towers of St. Basil's Cathedral in Moscow.

School & Sports

Almost all Russians can read and write. Russian children aged 6 to 17 go to school six days a week. But they only have classes from September through May. Young people who pass an entrance exam can attend college for free.

Russians also enjoy sports. They play ice hockey, go skiing, and skating. They play basketball, baseball, and enjoy chess. Soccer is the most popular sport.

Like most people today, Russians love soccer.

The Moscow Subway system carries more passengers than any other subway in the world.

Transportation

Very few Russians own cars. But most cities have buses, subways, and other forms of public transportation. Railroads carry cargo, since highways don't reach all of Russia's vast area. Many rivers are frozen for much of the year, so travel by ship is limited.

Moscow's subway system is decorated with stained glass windows, grand statues, and mosaics. Mosaics are pictures made of tiny colored glass tiles.

Unusual Places

About one-fifth of all the fresh water on Earth is in a lake in Siberia. Lake Baikal is the deepest lake in the world. It is nearly a mile deep. It is fed by 336 rivers and streams. Thanks to tons of tiny crayfish that eat water plants and bacteria, Lake Baikal is very clear. There are plants and animals in the lake that you can't find anywhere else.

Although it is located hundreds of miles from the nearest ocean, Lake Baikal has seals. Scientists do not yet know how seals, who usually live in seawater, first came to the lake.

Since 1992, Lake Baikal and the beautiful surrounding forest have become a national park where people enjoy hiking, bird watching, boating, and fishing.

Visiting the Country

In the center of Red Square is a big red-and-black pyramid that holds the remains of Vladimir Lenin. People come to look at the body inside the glass box, and to pay their respects to the man who led the Russian Revolution.

This was the first dog in space.

Window to the Past

The Russians had the first space program. They sent probes to the planets Venus and Mars.

On October 4, 1957, the Russians launched the first man-made Earth satellite, *Sputnik*. A satellite is an object that orbits the Earth. Just a month later, the Russians sent a dog into orbit. That satellite was nicknamed "Muttnik."

In 1986, the Russians launched the first permanent space station, Mir. Mir means Peace. Mir stayed in space until 2001.

Now the Russians have joined the United States and other countries to build the International Space Station.

In 1963, Valentina Tereshkova became the first woman in space.

On April 12, 1961, Yuri Gagarin became the first man to orbit the Earth.

In 1977, the complete body of a 6 to 8 month old baby mammoth was found in northeastern Siberia.

X-tra Special Things

Nesting dolls are very popular around the world.

Have you ever been to the circus? Russia has had many. They train many animals, including bears, lions, dogs, and pigs.

Peter Carl Faberge was a Russian goldsmith who made the world's most expensive eggs.

Some of the best gymnasts in the world come from Russia.

One of the special things in Russia is the nesting doll. It is also called **Matreshka**, which means "Little Mothers." The first doll was made by artist Sergei Maliutin in 1890. It can be seen in the Museum of Russian and Foreign Toys.

In Siberia and Alaska, there are several **mammoths**. They were found frozen. These huge, hairy, elephants are over 10,000 years old.

May Day started as an ancie[nt] celebration of spring. Now i[t] is also a national holiday an[d] gives people the chance to wear folk costumes.

Yearly Festivals

Under Communism, Christmas, Easter, and folk festivals were replaced by national holidays. Now Russians are celebrating religious holidays again.

Shrovetide takes place just before Lent. During Lent, Christians give up meat and other treats. Shrovetide celebrates the arrival of spring. At a big carnival, Russians burn a straw figure representing winter. Then they eat a feast of **bliny**, which are fluffy Russian pancakes.

Sabantui is another celebration in which Islamic Russians enjoy silly races, wrestling, and other contests. Children are given painted eggs and sweets.

А	И	Р	Ш
Б	Й	С	Щ
В	К	Т	Ъ
Г	Л	У	Ы
Д	М	Ф	Ь
Е	Н	Х	Э
Ё	О	Ц	Ю
Ж	П	Ч	Я
З			

Z

Russian is written with the Cyrillic alphabet. Cyrillic was based on the ancient Greek alphabet. The original Cyrillic alphabet had 43 letters. The modern Russian alphabet has 33. Though it has letters that can make the Z sound, the Cyrillic alphabet has no letter Z.

Let's try to say a Russian word. Rot means mouse. Roll your tongue as you say it; *Rrrote.* In Russian, mouse is spelled роt.

■ Russian and English Words

antler (ANT-lur) one of a pair of branched horns that grow on the heads of some deer

balalaika (BA-lah-LYE-kah) a guitar-like Slavic stringed instrument

bliny (blee-NEE) thin Russian pancakes often filled with cheese or fruit

borsch (borsh) a Russian or Polish soup made mostly from beets and cabbage

caviar (KA-vee-awr) salted eggs of the sturgeon

Communist (KOM-yuh-nist) a form of government in which property is shared

czar (ZAR) a Russian emperor

dacha (DAH-cha) a Russian country house or cottage

dvigatel' (DVEE-goh-tel) Russian word for an engine

Kremlin a fort within a Russian city, such as The Kremlin in Moscow, which houses the Russian government

landlord (LAND-lord) someone who rents his land or buildings to others for profit

mammoth (MAM-uhth) a large, shaggy Ice Age elephant

matreshka (ma-TRROH-shka) Russian nesting dolls

odezhda (oh-DEZH-dah) Russian word for clothing

peasant (PEZ-uhnt) a farmer who works for a landlord or owns a small farm

reindeer (RAYN-dihr) a large deer that lives in the far north, called caribou in North America

reka (ree-KAH) Russian word for river

revolution (rev-uh-LOO-shun) a violent change of government (or other big change)

shrovetide (SHROVE-tide) the four days before Lent

Soviet (SOH-vee-et) a council of workers, peasants, or other people

tsar' (ZAR) the Russian word for emperor

tusk (TUHSK) one of a pair of long teeth that stick out of the closed mouth of certain animals, like walruses

ushanka (oo-SHAHN-kah) a warm Russian hat with ear flaps

zhivotnoe (zhi-VOHT-noh-yeh) Russian word for animal

■ Let's Explore More

Look What Came From Russia by Miles Harvey, Franklin Watts, 1999

Peter the Great by Diane Stanley, Morrow Junior, 1999

The Magic Nesting Doll by Jacqueline K. Ogburn, Dial Books for Young Readers, 2000

A Look at Russia (Our World) by Helen Frost, Pebble Books, 2001

Websites

www.peacecorps.gov/kids/world/europemed/russia.html
Learn about the Russian land, food, holidays, and what kids do for fun.

http://library.thinkquest.org/CR0212302/russia.html
Learn about Russia and life in Russia from a 10-year-old Russian girl.

Index

Italic page numbers indicate illustrations.

Meet the Authors

JUSTINE & RON FONTES have written nearly 400 children's books together. Since 1988, they have published *critter news*, a free newsletter that keeps them in touch with publishers from their home in Maine.

The Fonteses have written many biographies and early readers, as well as historical novels and other books combining facts with stories. Their love of animals is expressed in the nature notes columns of *critter news*.

During his childhood in Tennessee, Ron was a member of the Junior Classical League and went on to tutor Latin students. At 16, Ron was drawing a science fiction comic strip for the local newspaper. A professional artist for 30 years, Ron has also been in theater as a costumer, makeup artist, and designer.

Justine was born in New York City and worked in publishing while earning a BA in English Literature Phi Beta Kappa from New York University. Thanks to her parents' love of travel, Justine visited most of Europe as a child, going as far north as Finland. During college, she spent time in France and Spain.